PET OWNER'S GUIDE TO THE
STAFFORDSHIRE
BULL TERRIER

Clare Lee
Photography: Keith Allison

RINGPRESS

D0349213

ABOUT THE AUTHOR

Clare Lee was brought up with Staffordshire Bull Terriers. Her father owned the famous Constones kennel, and she went into partnership with him and her husband in the 1960s. Today, Constones is the oldest active kennel in the UK, with all its stock tracing back in a direct line to a bitch purchased by her father in 1942. The Lees have owned and bred many top-winning Staffords, the foremost being Ch. Constones Yer Man, who broke the breed record when he won his 19th Challenge Certificate, and was Best of Breed at the Centenary Crufts Dog Show in 1991. Clare is a international Championship judge; she has judged Staffords at Crufts and has travelled worldwide on judging appointments.

ACKNOWLEDGEMENTS

I would like to thank all the people who helped with this book, those who supplied photos, and especially those who gave their time – and were very patient – at the photographic sessions. Chief among these: Russell Marsh, Simon Hinchcliffe, Pam Smith, Harriett, Alice and Eliza Williamson, Rosemary Jackson, Gerry Holmes, Clive Couling, the Simmons family, Sharon Fletcher, John and Susan Chesters, John Turner, Chris and Carmella Mudd, and Shirley and Adrian Whiteman. Thanks also to Knaresbrough Dog Training Club and Val Rodgers for help with the agility equipment, to Les Lacey and Josh, and to Alan Raymond for allowing the use of his photograph to illustrate the Breed Standard. Finally, my thanks to my husband, Tony, for ideas, encouragement, and much-needed help with the proof-reading.

Published by Ringpress Books,
A Division of INTERPET LTD,
Vincent Lane, Dorking, Surrey, RH4 3YX

First published 1998
This reprint 2008
© Interpet Publishing. All rights reserved

ISBN 978 1 86054 082 0

Printed in China through Printworks Int. Ltd.

CONTENTS

Introducing
The Stafford

Since earliest times one canine descendant of the wolf has been especially identified by its size, breadth of head, shortness of muzzle, strength of jaw and outstanding courage. Mainly used for hunting large game such as wild boar, this dog also had a role as a warrior dog. Just such a dog was to be found fighting alongside the Ancient Britons against the Roman invaders.

ENTERTAINMENT

The Romans were so impressed with these dogs, whom they called 'Pugnaces' or 'broad-mouthed' dogs, that some were sent to Rome to be used for the sporting entertainments that so delighted Roman crowds. Their bloodlines featured in the later development of many of the larger European breeds and, at the time of the Norman Conquest, they could be found taking part in bull, bear and even lion baiting.

BULL BAITING

Bear and bull baiting reached the height of popularity from the middle of the 16th century through to the middle of the 17th century when very large and powerful dogs were required to 'throw' the bull. From the end of the 17th century it became more popular to tether the bull and a somewhat smaller bull dog was developed. This 'bulldog' was leggier, lighter and altogether quicker than his modern cousin. The head, however, is not dissimilar and had been expertly evolved by selective breeding for the specific task to hand. To enable the dog to pin the bull by the nose and hang on for a long time, the under-jaw was hugely developed while a top jaw that lay back was bred for, so that the nostrils were not obstructed. It is even thought that the wrinkles on the face were selectively bred in so that blood (and a nose wound would bleed heavily) could run off the dog's face and not into his eyes.

THE SPORTING DOG

This Bulldog is the first direct ancestor of our Staffordshire Bull Terrier. As bull baiting became less popular, dog fighting enjoyed a sudden surge of interest towards the end of the 18th century. Men who had been famous for the prowess of their bull baiting dogs began to gain recognition as owners of fine fighting dogs. Such a man was Ben White from Shepherds Market, London, who fought his dogs in most of the pits in the City.

Some modification of the dog was necessary. The Bulldog was bred to pin and hang on at all costs – exciting enough when he was pitched against an animal of the magnitude and ferocity of a bull, but boring in the extreme when pitched against another dog. The muzzle needed to lose its lay back and the teeth to become larger – so that different grips could occur and plenty of blood could flow. All, would you believe, in order to titillate the crowd. While these modifications could have been successfully obtained by selective breeding from the existing Bulldog stock, it seems

more likely that some terrier blood was introduced. The name given to this type of dog – Bull-and-Terrier – supports this latter theory. The Bull-and-Terrier, or Pit Terrier, was a quick but strong dog with a longer muzzle than the earlier Bulldog. Apart from dog fighting, he was mainly used for ratting and badger baiting.

With such a bloody history you might wonder how this dog could have become the very popular family pet that it undoubtedly is today. It should be noted that the key requirement for the type of dog from which the Stafford stems was that it must, above all else, possess great courage. Even the rules of dog fighting tipped the scales in favour of the courageous dog – the one who would not give up, who kept coming up to the scratch line – rather than towards the most aggressive animal.

Furthermore, these pastimes, especially the fighting, necessitated a great deal of human contact. After each round the dogs had to be broken, picked up and taken back to their corners. Contemporary prints of the Westminster Pit show the handlers with their sleeves rolled up and arms completely unprotected ready to go in and pick up the dogs – these men were certainly

Enthusiasm for the new breed was centred on the Midlands in the UK.

not expecting the dogs to bite them. The ability to distinguish between animal and human is one of the most endearing and obvious characteristics of the Staffordshire Bull Terrier.

Although these barbaric pastimes were patronised by the sporting aristocracy – Lord Camelford owned a famous fighter called Belcher – fighting dogs were also owned by the lowliest families. In these households the dogs were useful ratters but could also earn money when worked against badgers or when put to fighting. It was often reported that the children of such families were deprived of food when it was necessary to give all the best victuals to the wage-earning dog. Pampered as they were within the family, they lived cheek by jowl with the humans. It was certainly their ability to fit into the family circle which prevented them from becoming extinct after the outlawing of dog fighting and before they were recognised as a pure and separate breed of dog.

Dog fighting was outlawed in 1835 and during the following hundred years, where fighting occurred, it was strictly 'underground'.

THE MODERN STAFFORD

While our Bull-and-Terriers, in little pockets throughout the country, were getting their paws planted firmly under tables, with an occasional foray into more nefarious pastimes, important developments were going on elsewhere.

In Birmingham, James Hinks, an exceptionally far-sighted dog breeder, was perfecting a new variety. He bred the Bull-and-Terrier to the Old English White Terrier, added a dash of Dalmatian and succeeded in producing an elegant, all-white dog known simply as the Bull Terrier. It quickly caught the attention of the dog-showing fraternity and, in the first Stud Book issued by the Kennel Club in 1874, 115 Bull Terriers (all sizes) are listed. Physically, these dogs were far removed from their Bulldog ancestors, having longer heads and tiny, triangular eyes.

Nevertheless, the courage and tenacity of the Bulldog could not be quenched.

There seems to have been something of a social divergence at this point. The Bull Terriers attracted a higher-class owner than the older Bull-and-Terriers, and these latter were officially christened the Staffordshire Bull Terrier in 1935.

Kennel Club acceptance of the Staffordshire as a pure breed probably had as much to do with Bull Terrier breeders than any effort on the part of Stafford fanciers. For some years prior to recognition, Bull Terrier people had been using canine older cousins in matings to produce a coloured variety of the Bull Terrier. Puppies from these litters with the longest heads and the smallest eyes were taken to be Bull Terriers and the rest were left to be included in the general melting pot of the Bull-and-Terrier. Staffords appeared in advertisements or in dog publications as a variety of Bull Terrier, the poor relation of their show-winning cousins. Breeders of the Bull Terrier were anxious to draw a distinction between the two breeds and this possibly explains the strange fact that the breed was recognised by the Kennel Club before an official Standard or breed club was established. Since so many of this type of dog existed in and around the Black Country in the Midlands, it was appropriate that the first meetings with a view to getting the breed recognised should take place there and that the name finally chosen for the Bull-and-Terrier should be The Staffordshire Bull Terrier.

Many problems faced the new breed, which was a mixture of pure bred and Bull Terrier cross animals. Even by 1939, of the fifteen Staffords who had won entry into the Kennel Club Stud Book, six had either one or both parents unregistered.

BREED CLUBS

The first club show for the breed was held in August 1935 in the Midlands at Cradley Heath, where sixty dogs and bitches were entered. In 1937 fanciers in the London area got together and started a club for the South of England and today there are eighteen breed clubs from the North of Scotland to the West Country, including Northern Ireland.

The fame of the breed has spread abroad. First exports naturally went to countries where British people had settled: Australia, South Africa and the USA. These countries have thriving Stafford Clubs and produce very good entries at shows. More recently, the breed has increased in popularity in Europe where Stafford fraternities are established in Eire, Finland, Germany, Austria, Holland, Spain, Belgium, Sweden, Norway and Denmark with a good transfer of

A breed of great courage.

11

judges, ideas and animals occurring between them and the country of origin.

Championship status was granted to the breed in 1938 and the first Challenge Certificates were awarded at the Birmingham National Dog Show in that year. The first champions of the breed, both born and bred in the Midlands, were Ch. Gentleman Jim and Ch. Lady Eve, who finished their Championships at the Bath Show in 1939. To get championship show status, breeders of the day had to work hard to reach a total of 750 registered Staffords. In 1996 registrations stood at 8,251 and at championship shows Staffords regularly produce the most entries of all the terrier breeds.

Staffordshire Bull Terriers have come a long way in their short history. Thanks to the efforts of their faithful admirers and their own excellent character they have now found a niche for themselves in almost every sphere of the dog world. They are occasional winners of the coveted Best in Show awards, beating much longer-established breeds. They have won Obedience Championships and have been accepted for training by charities such as Pets As Therapy to work as PAT dogs. Above all, they have proved themselves eminently suitable as family pets.

The Stafford is hardy, fun-loving and fearless.

BREED CHARACTERISTICS

The Staffordshire Bull Terrier was bred as a fighting dog, and Stafford enthusiasts are proud of the breed's colourful history. However, it is important to evaluate the characteristics that have been deliberately bred into the Stafford in order to see how they affect his performance as a companion dog, and whether he will be suitable for you and your family.

COURAGE

The most important characteristic of all the ancestors of the Stafford was their great courage. Aggression was necessary in a fighting dog – but, whereas a dog can be trained and conditioned to be aggressive, nothing can teach him courage. That is bred in him at birth. Breeders today value the courage of their dogs. Nobody is proud to own a timid Stafford, but no sensible breeder encourages aggression towards other animals. Responsible owners and breeders deliberately avoid confrontational experiences.

Courage is important in a pet dog because more dogs bite out of fear than for any other reason. A dog who is not easily alarmed can cope much better with the rough

Staffords get on well with children.

and tumble of a busy family home, one of the reasons the Stafford is such a success as a dog for children. He is as hardy and fun-loving, and fearless, as they are.

The Stafford represents, more than any other breed, the 'survival of the fittest' theory – history would surely have weeded out the weaker animals – and experienced beeders aim to keep up this tradition. A vet once complained that if he saw all his patients as often as he saw our dogs he would be bankrupt.

RECKLESSNESS

Of course, there is a down side. There is a fine line between fearlessness and foolhardiness. A Stafford owner can never afford to take the risk of underestimating what his or her dog is capable of attempting. 'He will not jump out of that window, crash through that fence, scale that wire' – all these assumptions can end in disaster for dog and owner. Tenacity is another key element of the fighting dog character. This can be another word for plain pigheadedness and, if a Stafford sets his mind to something, he will risk hell and high water to do it. This is the modern equivalent of the dog that will never give up the fight. Most tasks that dogs perform for man require the dog to follow instructions. In the fighting situation the dog has to think for himself – his very existence may depend upon it. This tendency to work things out and act on his own inclinations is a characteristic that all potential Stafford owners must be aware of and be ready to counteract, by thinking ahead in any situation.

AFFINITY WITH PEOPLE

Staffords are large-hearted and their way of showing that they love human beings does not express itself by a friendly wag of the tail and a gentle lick of the tongue. This is a dog that will launch itself at visitors, and even when trained to be more controlled, will still be a fussy pet – nudging and pawing the object of his affection in order to win a stroke and a pat in response. If you want a quiet reserved dog who 'knows his place' and will wait to be asked to join in the game, then a Stafford is not for you. It is recorded that fighting dogs often changed hands – to settle debts or simply to raise funds, but whatever the causes it is a well-known fact that Staffords are amazingly adaptable at changing home or even owners. Unfortunately, this does make them easy prey for 'dognappers', from whom they will need protection.

STRENGTH

Staffords are physically extremely strong for their size. They can bruise your legs if they try to barge past you, can be extraordinarily powerful if allowed to pull on a lead and, if left unsupervised and lonely, amazingly destructive in the home.

14

AGGRESSION

Finally, deep down inside them, is the in-bred possibility of fighting with other dogs. The motto generally taken by most Stafford Clubs is that of the Scottish kings – 'nemo me impune lacisset'. Roughly translated, this means that 'no one can attack me without getting back as good as I'm given'. No responsible Stafford owner will fail to remember that, if attacked, even the quietest Stafford could respond and fight back. Because of their power, their build and their history, they can do a lot more damage than their size would suggest.

Of course there are those people who will actively seek out the sort of dog they hope will beat up all the other dogs in the neighbourhood. If you feel that you are such a person then this breed is definitely not for you, as you would only bring a good breed into disrepute. Modern society is not willing to accept anti-social behaviour from dogs. Irresponsible owners undo all the hard work that generations of genuine lovers of the breed have expended in civilising it, while retaining all the characteristics that make the Stafford such a special and rewarding dog to own.

The Stafford is strong for its size.

2 Choosing A Stafford

Before any family buys a new car, a washing machine or makes any large addition to their household, its members will undoubtedly do some homework first. They will have a pretty clear idea of what is required for their particular family and they will take pains to select the model which has most of the features they desire. If only people would spend as much time and thought when selecting a dog for their family!

Unfortunately, many people buy a dog on a whim. They may see a photograph of a dog and 'fall in love' with its face, or may be swayed by the fact that a breed is used in a favourite advertisement. There is usually an upsurge in demand for any breed that wins Best in Show at Crufts. Some choose a breed to reflect the image they wish to portray, and when that image changes they look for another dog. There are also a number of families who fear, or have suffered, burglaries and think

that a dog is the answer to their security problems. But a dog is a living, sentient being who will be totally dependant upon you for ten to twelve years. A pedigree dog will be expensive to buy and costly to maintain, so it is surely worthwhile taking time to do some careful research before rushing out to buy a puppy.

The Staffordshire Bull Terrier is a medium-sized, strongly-built dog with a sturdy constitution and short, close coat. His temperament is lively and happy-go-lucky and he can adapt himself to a wide variety of households, providing his owners give him plenty of love and attention, and are blessed with a sense of humour! However, the Stafford does tend to be intolerant of other animals, especially any that challenge him. Care must be taken to avoid confrontational experiences, and to maintain a responsible attitude when exercising your dog. In return, the Stafford will give his family endless love, loyalty, and amusement.

MISCONCEPTIONS

I have found that there are three common reasons for people being dissatisfied with their choice of a Stafford as a pet. The first is that they have expected a dog who will sit in his basket and not demand fussing. The Stafford craves attention, is unhappy and can be a nuisance if deprived of close human companionship.

The second cause for dissatisfaction arises where the owner has expected his dog to run in the park and submit to even the biggest bully in that park, which the Stafford is unlikely to do.

Finally, there is a negative cause for complaint which stems from a misunderstanding about 'guarding'. The Stafford was not developed as a watchdog – he rarely barks, greets all your visitors and may well let them walk off with the family silver. If you want a dog to repel or at least be suspicious of all comers, then choose the breeds that have been especially designed for this purpose and can most easily and safely be trained to perform this task. Staffords may 'guard' their car, but rarely their owner's home.

They do, however, have an innate desire to protect their family. We have even known fathers who have been unable to chastise their children when the Stafford is around. Staffords do not need to be trained for this task; once accepted as a family member, they have an instinct to protect the weaker members of that family.

If you still feel attracted to the breed and you are confident that you have the correct environment for one, how do you set about purchasing a Staffordshire Bull Terrier?

BUYING A STAFFORD

It is always advisable to buy a pedigree dog, of whatever breed, directly from a recognised breeder. It is especially important in the case of the Staffordshire Bull Terrier. Every week the pets columns of local papers will include advertisements for Staffords from unregistered stock, cross-breeds and an increasing number of different 'types' of Stafford. Some of these dogs may make excellent pets but, equally, a lot will fall far short of a proper Staffordshire Bull Terrier. Secretaries of breed clubs are dealing with an increasing number of queries, complaints and cries for help from people who have purchased dogs via such adverts. These dogs, and their progeny, cannot be registered. There is only one breed called the Staffordshire Bull Terrier and it is recognised world-wide under the same Standard.

Of course it would be foolish to claim that all pups bought from recognised breeders will turn out to be show dogs, but a reputable breeder is attempting to breed to the recognised Standard. A pedigree is nothing more than names on a piece of paper unless it is backed by Kennel Club registration.

Your national Kennel Club will supply you with details of breed clubs. Make up your mind that you are not going to be in a hurry. A suitable litter may not be ready exactly at the time you enquire, so you may have to be patient. Take the opportunity to visit dog shows, which will provide you and your family with a chance to get some 'hands on ' experience of the breed. You may find breeders who, even if they have no puppies themselves, will let you visit their

A male will rarely live in harmony with another male dog.

Bitches are gentle and adaptable.

homes and meet their dogs – a golden opportunity for you to get to know what Staffords are like to live with.

Large commercial kennels of Staffords just do not exist. Ninety-nine per cent of Staffords, even in the most successful of show kennels, are living in the home with the family. There is nowhere you can visit rows of kennels full of mothers and pups in this breed.

DOG OR BITCH?

Before you finally start to visit

litters – and it is certainly an idea to see more than one litter if you possibly can – decide which sex you want. A male Stafford is a great character, which also means that he is very determined and will undertake amazing feats of daring if given the chance. Males are more muscular and stronger than bitches and therefore, if they get

White and red Stafford.

20

Black and white: Colour is a matter of personal preference.

into a tussle with another dog, they can inflict more damage. It is never wise to keep a male Stafford with another male of any breed and, in fact, it is almost impossible for two male Staffords to live together peaceably, unless there is a terrific age gap.

Bitches are generally more gentle. Although they can be very mischievous, they tend to have a greater sense of self-preservation, and are often greedier, than the males. Given love and friendship, they tend to take to new homes more easily than dogs. Females may well be as intolerant of other animals as the males but they are easier to separate from a foe. Bitches will have regular 'heats' or 'seasons' which some people find intolerable, and we deal with this in a later chapter.

COLOUR

You may have a preference for a particular colour. Very few breeders keep all the colours, but occasionally a litter of mixed red and brindle or, more commonly, coloured and pied litters occur. There is no real difference between the colours – it is a purely cosmetic preference. In general, breeders are known for one particular colour and, if you have a preference, you should state this from the outset when making enquiries about a pup.

CHOOSING YOUR PUPPY

When you go to see a litter it is

The temperament of the puppies' mother is all-important.

important to see the mother. If the breeder of the pups is unwilling to show you the mother, or the bitch seems of doubtful temperament, then beware; the pups will learn their first lessons about humans from the way their mother reacts. It follows that pups are much more likely to be suspicious of human beings if she is. If, of course, you are invited to see a very young litter – before their eyes are open for example – then you must expect the mother to be protective of them. A sensible breeder would never invite a stranger to view a litter at such an early stage, but it does sometimes happen, and in such a case I would be suspicious of the breeder's experience.

It is unlikely, but not impossible, that you will be able to see the father. Nearly always, breeders will have to travel some distance to find the best possible sire for their particular bitch. If you visit a few dog shows, you may be able to see the father of the pups at one of these.

WHAT TO LOOK FOR

Any litter of Stafford pups should be eager to come out of the box and run up to you. In fact, they will throw themselves at you, grab hold of your trouser bottoms and almost certainly attack your shoelaces within the first two minutes of your arrival. For this reason, I suggest that you go sensibly dressed. I have seen a pair of black tights shredded before my eyes within minutes of the elegant lady being introduced to a litter of eight-week-old puppies. If kept in the house, the pups will have the advantage of having already met many common household noises: televisions, vacuum cleaners, telephones, doorbells etc. They are also more likely to have been handled by the family and to have been fully socialised. This again is a great advantage for their future mental development. Puppies kept outside need not be disadvantaged if the breeder has played with them and handled them several times every day. Sometimes though, especially if the breeder is very busy and the pups are outside, it is easy to feed and clean thoroughly but to neglect playing with the pups, resulting in pups left on their own for hours at a time. Such puppies can get over this initial bad start, but it will mean a harder job for you. Should there be more than one litter, the job of socialising so many puppies is even harder and you may find the puppies reluctant to come to you, tentative and cringing. Never be tempted to pick the timid, tiny, poorly-looking pup, as you may be buying yourself a lot of heartache.

Physically, not all puppies are born to be champions of the show ring – in fact, very few will be so. However, they can all be healthy. Look for shining coats, bright eyes, well-covered bodies. If the puppies have distended, balloon-like stomachs, they probably have not been wormed properly. Worms are present in almost all puppies but, if they are not removed early and efficiently, they can cause

serious damage and restrict healthy growth.

The place where the puppies are kept should be scrupulously clean, as puppies allowed to play in their own faeces will not prosper. However, if you happen to see a pup performing, do not look away. Firm, well-formed, medium-brown droppings are a good sign that the pup has been receiving a correct well-balanced diet.

Good puppies will sell themselves, so, if you think that you are getting too much of a sales pitch, wonder why. Having said this, breeders are usually proud of their dogs and like to tell you all about the breeding line. Champions are often written in red or in capital letters on the

At eight weeks old, the breeder will be able to assess conformation.

Watch the puppies at play to discover their individual characters.

pedigree and it is usual to abbreviate this title to Ch. The father of a pup is called the sire and mother the dam. You can check on a pedigree through a breed club – phoney pedigrees are not uncommon, although they should be picked up by the Kennel Club when the pups' registration is applied for.

Whatever age you view the puppies, they should not be allowed to leave their mother until they are seven, and preferably eight, weeks old. By this time, they will be fully weaned and have had a chance to learn the important lessons that any good mother will teach her puppies.

You must be prepared to be vetted by the breeder. A genuine breeder will be anxious that his or her pup is going to a suitable home and will want to know about your family and lifestyle. Do not be offended. Indeed, if the only question is 'where is your money?', then consider walking away. You are unlikely to get any after-service from such a breeder.

Breeders who care like to hear news of the pup and to receive photos and a visit if possible. They should also be willing to help with any problems, or if your circumstances change and you have to re-home the pup at a later date.

THE PEDIGREE

The breeder should give you a signed pedigree with three, and preferably five, generations together with the registration form issued by the Kennel Club. The breeder should sign the back of this form so that you can have the pup transferred to your ownership.

At present, the breeder is the only person entitled to register the litter. Puppies must be registered within twelve months of birth, after which it is both difficult and costly to gain registration. Even if the parents are registered you will not be able to register a puppy without the breeder's signature and consent. If one or both of the parents are unregistered, you will not be able to register the puppies.

If the pup has had any inoculations, you should be given the veterinary card giving details and signed by the vet. In addition, you should be given a diet sheet and a note of the date on which the puppy was last wormed. Really good breeders will give you a sample of the food and possibly a blanket or something from the litter's home which will help the puppy settle into his new surroundings.

ONE AT A TIME

Puppies are most attractive little creatures and it can be very tempting to take two from a litter. Even if you choose one of each sex, this is not a good idea.

It may be tempting to buy two puppies – but you will end up with double the trouble.

Training a puppy is a hard job and two will get into (at least) twice as much mischief as one. There is nothing like the 'one to one' experience on walks or during training sessions for creating a bond between you and your dog, and you cannot get the same degree of bonding where you have two of the same age. It is far better to buy one, and when it is fully mature and trained, have another if you still wish – of the opposite sex if you want to avoid problems.

Staffords are not good with other dogs and they do not need them for company. It is your company and attention that they need. One of the most common reasons for two Staffords falling out in any household is jealousy.

They are so determined to have human love and attention that they can be insanely jealous of any other dog sharing your love.

CHOOSING A RESCUE DOG

Finally, if you decide that you want a family pet but cannot face the trauma of training a puppy, you might consider a rescue dog. The Stafford fraternity, as a whole, maintains a number of breed rescue organisations – your local breed club will advise and recommend you to one of these. They will want to check on you and your home. The rescue animal must be neutered, and good organisers will attempt to match your home conditions with the temperament and background of the individual dog.

3 *Puppy Care*

Before you bring the new puppy home, it is wise to make a few preparations. In the first place, decide where the pup will sleep. He may well cry for the first night, having never slept other than surrounded by four or five warm bodies. You will notice how a litter of puppies sleep in a big heap, piled on top of one another – they actually compete to be the one on the bottom. At this stage the danger is that you will be tempted to take the pup to bed with you 'just for tonight'. No breed appreciates a warm bed and the close proximity of a human body more than a Staffordshire Bull Terrier. If anyone were to take a census of the breeds that sleep in their owner's bed, I would hazard a guess that the Stafford would come top of the list; and it must be added that they are not content to lie on top of the bed but dive right under the covers. I had a friend who shared a normal double bed with his wife, a large Stafford dog, a Stafford bitch and a cat! This is not a sleeping arrangement that I would recommend.

GETTING READY

You can buy dog bowls in readiness. Plastic ones are fine, but, left alone, the puppy can, and will, chew it to a frilly pattern around the edge. Metal bowls are not indestructible, but certainly last longer. Water bowls must be spill-proof and, if they are made of pottery, must be very heavy. We have had personal experience of a young Stafford playing 'throw the water bowl' and finishing up with a very serious cut requiring several stitches.

Next, take a walk around your garden. A well-fenced garden is essential for a Stafford. Check that there are no gaps in or under the fence – a pup can get through amazingly small spaces – and Staffords are not afraid to tackle hedges of any description. Gates

Your puppy will feel bewildered when he first arrives home.

are potential hazards. Very often they have a big gap at the bottom and, if they give access for dustbin men, window cleaners etc., put a lock on them. It is so easy for gates to be accidentally left open and the pup could get out to be run over or stolen.

Decide on the house rules as far as the dog is concerned – and stick to them! It is tempting to allow a little pup, with tiny, clean paws, to sit on the furniture, but come the day a bigger pup with filthy, muddy paws jumps on your sofa there is trouble! The pup will not understand the difference between clean and dirty feet and it is confusing for him to be allowed to do something on one day and be chastised for doing the same thing on the next.

ARRIVING HOME

When you go to collect your pup take a towel and a pile of newspapers in case he is sick on the journey home. The breeder should give you the pedigree, registration form, diet sheet and the inoculation certificate, if applicable.

Once home, the pup will be uncertain and a bit bewildered by the new scenery – all his former points of reference have been taken away. He will need a quiet period to adapt to his new home. This is why it is important not to introduce a pup at Christmas time when there is so much noise and activity and strange people coming in and out of the house.

If you already have other animals in the household, introduce the new pup with care and consideration, and do not let the incumbent pet feel that he must take second place to the newcomer. Staffords brought up with cats, horses, rabbits etc. can be exemplary in their behaviour towards these additional members of the family, as long as care is taken to make the introductions properly and control is maintained. You must be the overall boss of the family and avoid over-exciting the Stafford in games with other pets.

The most important requirement for the bed is that it is draught-free and in a warm place. Staffords have very short, close coats and therefore have no defence against harsh weather. Buy a sensible basket – duvets, cushions, bean bags and pretty wicker baskets may be fine when he is older but, during the early months and when teething, the pup chews a lot, so it is better to opt for a strong, plastic basket

which can also be easily washed. Inside the basket you can put a piece of blanket, but most breeders prefer the fleecy synthetic Vet-Bed which allows moisture to permeate through and is easily laundered. If you are worried about the puppy crying, try a stone hot water bottle (he may chew a rubber one) covered in a towel or cloth. A ticking clock wrapped in a blanket may remind him of the heartbeats of his littermates and consequently soothe him.

Positioning the bed is also important. For the first few weeks, he will most likely be unable to

Allow your pup to explore the garden.

hold his water all night. Therefore put the basket on a washable surface, or protect the floor around his bed with copious amounts of newspaper. Place it where it does not interfere too much with the family and where he has easy access. Remember, the bed is your dog's home base. Respect his property. If he feels tired, unwell or just wants a rest from people, he will retire to this bed and he should be allowed to rest there undisturbed.

Allow your puppy to explore the garden, staying with him and giving reassurance. Now is the time to choose your command for getting the pup to do his toilet. This can be: "Be clean, Busy" – the words do not matter. The important thing is to speak loudly and clearly – even if the neighbours are sunbathing in their garden – and to repeat the command until your dog can perform almost to order. Above all else, remember to praise effusively as soon as your pup does perform outside.

DAILY ROUTINE

Create a routine for the pup – he will feel secure within this framework and it will be easier both to house-train him and to keep him amused, reducing the opportunities for chewing and other destructive behaviour. The sort of routine and the type of feeding that I would employ for an eight-week-old puppy would be as follows:

- On waking – take your puppy outside and stay with him until he has relieved himself.
- Breakfast – give approx. $1/4$ pint milk mixed with cereal such as instant porridge, rusks or Weetabix.
- Take outside again to relieve himself.
- Playtime followed by rest period. Long periods of sleep are absolutely necessary for puppies. Every member of the family – especially the younger children – should be made to understand that a puppy needs these sleep periods if he is to grow properly and not to become fractious.
- Lunch – 3ozs of minced meat, or equivalent of tinned meat, together with some biscuit meal or small bite mixer, or dried puppy food.
- Take outside to relieve himself.
- Playtime followed by rest period.
- Tea – as lunch or, for a change, scrambled egg and a little cheese.

Puppies are used to feeding together, and may miss the rivalry of their littermates.

- Take outside to relieve himself.
- Supper – $^1/_4$ pint milk mixed with cereal or similar.
- Take outside and encourage to relieve himself.

PUPPY DIET

The quantity of food suggested in the Daily Routine is an average – a smaller pup or a larger one will eat correspondingly less or more. If you are feeding a mixed diet of your own concoction e.g. fresh mince and biscuit, you may be well advised to give some vitamin supplement. Cod liver oil is a favourite of many breeders but should be given with some form of Vitamin D if it is to be of use. If you are feeding proprietary brands of food and you are carefully following the directions on the can or package, then extra vitamins should not be necessary and, indeed, may be dangerous if given in too great a dosage. Fresh, clean water should be available at all times.

People worry whether they are giving the puppy enough food. It is never a good idea to save money either in quantity or quality for a young animal – building a sound, healthy foundation will stand him in good stead as a mature animal. One guide that you can easily follow is to keep an eye on the puppy's faeces – too hard and small, and you are indeed under-feeding; loose, you have probably given too much. Cutting down, or even cutting out just one meal in a day, can sort this problem out very quickly. Look at your puppy daily – are his eyes bright, is his coat shiny and does he appear to be well-covered with flesh and have plenty of energy? If the answer is yes, then what you are doing is right for your pup.

Any incidence of loose bowels should be watched carefully. If the simple act of cutting out one meal does not work and the loose motions continue, starve the pup for twenty-four hours, while still providing water to drink. Then make him a light meal of chicken and rice and continue with this diet until the motions are correct. A couple of arrowroot biscuits in water is a good substitute for his normal milky meals, as milk will only exacerbate the problem. If, after twenty-four hours you see no improvement, or if there has been a quantity of blood in his faeces, consult your vet.

If you do not want to feed the pup on the same type of food as the breeder, there is no problem as long as you follow the golden rule of making the change gradually – do not just change a pup's diet in one go as that will surely upset his stomach.

HOUSE TRAINING

Always take pup outside in the garden after eating and as soon as he wakes from a sleep – this way he will become house-trained without much hassle. In between times, if you see him going round in small circles, or sniffing in a generally unsettled way, or standing close to the outside door – take him outside quickly. If he does perform in the house, tell him he is naughty and show him immediately where he should have performed. It is important that you show him the correct place to go, or he will be confused and imagine that it is what he is doing, rather than where he is doing it, that is causing you displeasure.

A Stafford will very quickly catch on to the idea that you are displeased with him but it is important to show him the times that you are pleased with him too!

INOCULATIONS

Make an appointment to take the pup to the veterinary surgeon for his inoculations, and to discuss a worming routine, as soon as you can. Until the pup is fully immunised – two weeks after the last injection – he should not be taken for walks or allowed to sniff or play where strange dogs have been exercised.

It is a good idea to take him for short daily rides in the car at this stage as a lot of young Staffords suffer from car sickness, but they will usually outgrow this. Staffords generally love travelling and the car is one of the few possessions that they do seem to guard fiercely.

Dogs are immunised against distemper, hepatitis, leptospirosis, parvovirus and probably para-influenza. Some people, especially if showing or attending busy training classes, will also have their

Lessons on the lead should be started at an early stage.

dogs inoculated against kennel cough. Some boarding kennels ask for this vaccination.

EARLY LESSONS

While you are waiting for his inoculations to be completed, you can get your puppy used to wearing a collar for a short time during the day. You could also try walking him around the garden on a lead – this is not easy at first as the pup will probably buck and bounce or dig his heels in and refuse to move at all! Gentle coaxing – using a tidbit to encourage him forward – is the best way. Never drag him along, you can put him off the collar and lead and make your task of lead training him much harder. Be careful about letting any dog play with another when they are wearing collars – a tooth jammed in a collar can result in a squealing, choking pup.

Once it is safe to take the puppy out make sure that his collar is fairly tightly fastened. If frightened, his first instinct will be to go backwards and, if he manages to slip his collar, you may have a problem catching him again. You should just be able to slip your fingers between the collar and the dog's neck. Do not be tempted to go for too long a walk at first. The trouble with any Stafford is that he will keep going and never want to give in, so it is easy to over-walk a pup and you could well find him stiff or his paws bleeding the next morning. Until he is six months of age, a Stafford will need only short walks.

INDOOR CRATE

If you are concerned about damage to your house and furniture, then you might consider buying an indoor crate. When used for limited periods, a crate can be a useful aid to the dog owner, but problems arise if owners leave dogs for hours in these very cramped conditions. This is totally wrong. The crate should be viewed as a safe haven for your puppy – and he should be quite happy to be confined for a

A crate can also be used in the car.

Staffords thrive on companionship and should not be left alone for long periods.

family members are the two most common problems reported by new owners. Boredom is the major cause of chewing, but is intensified when he is losing his teeth at around four to five months old.

If you go out to work you must make arrangements for someone to come and spend some time with the puppy, to let him out and give him some freedom during the day. Going out for short periods and leaving the pup alone is good for him – he should be made to accept that he will be left alone at times.

Toys can be useful to keep the pup occupied. Balls should not be too big, but, then again, not so small that a young dog could swallow them. All rubber toys should be viewed with caution as a dog with the strength of jaw of the Stafford can chew small pieces off and swallow them, and these do not always show up on an X-ray. Nyla-bones and similar last longer than most toys.

Fresh bones can be very enjoyable but are frowned upon by vets, who see so many accidents as a result of puppies chewing bones. If you want to give a bone make sure that it is a large, marrow-type bone and

short time. The other advantage is that the crate is collapsible and so it can be used as a portable home if you are travelling. Many hotels are happy to accept a dog if it can be accommodated in a crate. One word of caution – puppies can get their jaws caught in the wires of some crates, so never use them for tiny pups.

PROVIDING STIMULATION
Chewing furniture and nibbling

As your puppy matures, he will become more assertive.

get hold of them, and never leave him unattended in your best living room.

Chewing fingers is the other great problem. Tiny puppies have teeth like needles which can prove very painful. Do not be afraid to make it clear to the pup that you are not his plaything nor a larger version of his littermates. In spite of modern ideas from canine psychiatrists about what we should or should not say to our dogs, my observations have led me to the conclusion that, at least where Staffords are concerned, those owners who give a decisive "No" and a sharp tap on the nose to a pup who is misbehaving seem to get their message over the quickest.

never cooked. Any bone that splinters is very dangerous and bones should not be given too often as they can cause constipation.

I cannot stress too strongly the amount of damage a bored, lonely Stafford pup can achieve – yards of door-frame, whole areas of vinyl flooring, complete sides of settees – these are just a few of the casualties I have come across. Never leave shoes, slippers, cardigans, etc. where the pup can

FAMILY PET

Staffords are renowned for making good family pets; they are rough and tough and therefore can put up with the rowdy behaviour of young children. They are not, however, indestructible and many accidents have occurred where young children have been allowed to pick up little pups who then struggle out of their arms. Sometimes no harm is done, but I have seen a jaw dislocated and limbs broken because a child has dropped a puppy. Teach the dog to respect the child by stopping him chewing and grabbing at his clothes, and teach the child to respect the dog by holding it only when the child is sitting down so that the pup has a very little distance to fall.

ADOLESCENCE
Having got through those first crucial weeks, the new owner tends to sit back, relax, and imagine that he or she and the pup will live 'happily ever after'. But, as the pup starts to lose his initial cute vulnerability and grows in confidence, he sprouts into a juvenile, and a new set of

problems may be just around the corner.

ADOLESCENT DIET
First there is the problem of diet. Many puppies start to lose interest in one or both of their milk meals at around twelve to fourteen weeks. This does not matter and, if you are afraid the pup looks thin, you can increase the biscuit content of his two meat meals. If he still seems happy with the breakfast and supper meals, and is not too 'roly poly', then keep giving them, or give them in a smaller amount. At nine months, most pups will be down to two meals – usually lunch and tea or, if

Games with children should be closely supervised.

it fits in better with your routine, breakfast and tea. It is usually better to drop the evening meal first as it helps the pup to go through the night without any accidents.

TEETHING
At around four to five months, the pup begins to lose his baby teeth and his second ones come through. The first teeth are like needles and very painful if he starts to play roughly with your fingers or ankles. Do not be afraid, even at this young age, to make it clear that you do not want to be nibbled and object to him hurting you. The second teeth, while less needle-like, are much stronger. His mouth will be very sore while these new teeth are breaking though the gums and his instinct will be to gnaw on any hard surface that he can find. If you have not supplied enough toys to chew, or have allowed him to chew slippers while he was young and the small teeth could do little harm, you will now begin to repent your folly. This is the time that the puppy's new, strong teeth help him to demolish the kitchen or chew through the table leg. There was a famous case of an owner of an antique table, who

resorted to sawing three legs down to match the one that his Stafford had chewed through. Now is the time you might have to think about using a cage – it is not too late to train the pup to use one. Supply plenty of legitimate things to chew, especially when you are out. Just remember, it is a phase that passes and things will get better in time.

SIDE EFFECTS
Around teething time, and if the dog is in low health, Staffords commonly lose hair, usually around the face, especially the eyes and behind the ears, inside the back legs and possibly in the middle of the tail. This is often diagnosed as mange and there are as many home cures for this condition as there are old wives' tales. These recommend anything from benzyl benzoate to engine oil as a 'sure fire' remedy. In fact, if left alone, the vast majority of youngsters will resist this mange mite all by themselves. Given good food and a little sunshine on their backs, the hair will eventually grow back as the pup's own metabolism fights off the condition. Severe cases should be referred to your veterinary surgeon and it must be said that even vets

sometimes have difficulty clearing up the problem.

PROBLEMS

While your pup is teething keep an eye on the progress of the teeth. The main thing is to note that the new teeth come in and push out the baby ones. It is easy to see the difference between these two sets of teeth as the baby ones appear very small and thin beside the second set. You should watch to see baby teeth come out or you may find that you have a double row of teeth, which can result in food becoming stuck between them and causing decay.

Another problem is that of in-growing canines. The canine teeth are the four large fangs at each side of the mouth top and bottom. So-called 'in-growing' or 'converging' canines is a condition where the lower canine teeth are set too far inside the jaw and press into the roof of the mouth. Most animals accommodate this but if the problem is acute it can cause pain, or at least discomfort, and may make the dog grumpy, so consult your vet.

4 Training Your Puppy

When you visit more experienced owners of Staffordshire Bull Terriers, there is often no obvious evidence of any training having been done at all with the Staffords in the house. You are unlikely to be greeted with a display of "Down" or "Sit" when you are introduced to the dog. Nor does it help to read books on dog psychology or training which stress that dogs are pack animals. One of the first things you will learn about your Stafford is that he thinks he is human and is most unlikely to want any part of this 'doggy pack' business.

However, it must be said that most Stafford breeders have very strong characters, which probably attracts them to this particular breed in the first place. The dog will have learnt from his owner at an early age what behaviour is acceptable and what is not. Thus the Stafford tends, chameleon-like, to take on the character of his particular family – if they are lively

and noisy he will be rushing up and down stairs and round the garden like a dervish. If they are quiet and tidy he will learn to sit, fairly neatly, by the fireside.

STARTING RIGHT

A dog of any breed needs to know his place in the community in which he lives and, most important of all, he needs to know who is 'boss' of that community. You need to make sure that the boss is yourself. The worst punishment that you can inflict on a Stafford is to ignore him. 'I don't like you, go away' causes more suffering than a smack, or worse, physical punishment. You must give praise when he does right and you must make it absolutely clear in the tone of your voice, in your stance, in the look in your eye that 'enough is enough and I will no longer tolerate this kind of behaviour'. It is not fashionable to use the word "No" but with a breed as headstrong as the Stafford, it is the word above all others, short and sharply delivered, that is most likely to pull them up in their tracks.

ESTABLISHING CONTROL

Much has been made in recent years of the theory of 'dominance' in the dog. Allowing, as I have said, that owners of the best Staffords are probably fairly strong characters themselves, they are often not aware of having taken any positive steps to be the dominant one in the relationship – the dog has just fitted in to the family. Where this has not been the case, the humans have been unassertive and haphazard in their treatment of the dog, or have expected untypical behaviour from the Stafford. I should mention the animals concerned have invariably been male.

There are a few 'tricks' to reinforce our dominance – not sharing your bed with the dog is one, although as already mentioned, numerous Stafford owners break this rule with no ill effects. I would recommend that you make sure that you are able to hoist the dog out of the bed if need be and, if you find that he is growling at you when you do this, never have him in the bed again.

One of the important words to teach all dogs is "Stay". Staffords are impetuous and will run out of a front door on to a busy road or through an inside door into a room where you may have a strange dog, wet paint etc. It is vital, therefore, that the dog learns to "stay" while the owner walks first through any door. This is also an important way of reinforcing dominance over the dog.

When the puppy is very young, and from time to time afterwards, take the opportunity to move his bowl, or take it away briefly, while he is feeding – just to make sure there is no adverse reaction. Also make sure that you can take a toy or some highly prized object out of the dog's mouth. Expect to be able to do this and to be able to pick up your Stafford and pull or push him off any chair without any fear of being bitten or, indeed, even being growled at. If there is any adverse reaction, jump on it quickly with a sharp rebuke. The younger the dog, the easier it is to start teaching these important lessons.

TRAINING CLASSES

If you do not have the confidence or experience to set rules for the dog, or if you feel you are 'losing

Your Stafford should learn basic commands such as "Sit."

"Stay" is an all-important command for your dog's future safety.

control', get in touch with your local dog training classes. All dogs benefit from knowing a few words of command, "Sit" and "Stay" being the minimum. These simple training classes will teach your dog a few basic rules but, much more importantly, will teach you to take the upper hand. It will boost your confidence and enrich the relationship between yourself and your dog. It is true that quite a few Staffords are now attending classes and attaining high degrees of competence in obedience tests –

one actually qualified to go to Crufts Obedience Competition. But even a basic level of training can help you and your Stafford to get along together. Some classes start very young with 'puppy socialising' classes where young pups can learn to play together. It can be lonely for a pup, used to playing with a number of littermates, to suddenly find himself separated from contact with other dogs, and he will enjoy the games. A word of warning. I have known Stafford puppies who

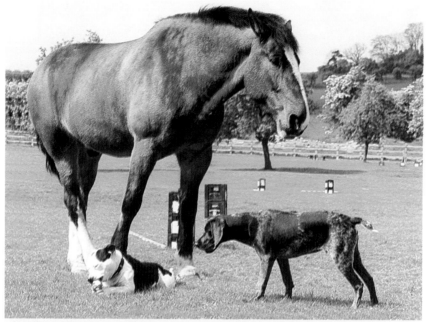

A well socialised dog will be calm and adaptable.

were banned from these classes because of complaints that they 'play too rough'. Therefore, choose your pup's playmates with care, and, if you are sent away in disgrace, you have not necessarily got a monster, it is just that the rest are not strong enough to cope with a Stafford's idea of play.

One form of training that a Stafford should never be given is any kind of 'man control' – that is, thief-catching exercises for which police dogs are trained. The development of the breed has been based on 'four legs bad but two legs good', so it could be dangerous to attempt to alter its natural inclinations.

OUT AND ABOUT

Once he has completed his course of inoculations, I cannot overstress the importance of taking the puppy out and about as much as possible. Staffords are extrovert, inquisitive animals, who need to meet people, traffic, bicycles, children etc. Take the puppy in the car. Take him into town. In general, I do not believe dogs and shopping sprees go together, but a busy public market is the perfect place to teach a young animal about the noises and stresses of modern living. Go, not to shop, but to educate the pup.

Your main problem will be that the Stafford will want to say 'hello' by jumping up and licking everyone he comes across. It needs a gentle touch to dissuade him from doing this without putting him off. Pull the pup back, say "No" and when he desists tell him he is a good boy. Most people will stroke him at this stage and so the whole thing should pass off with no harm done. If, every time he meets someone and goes up to them, you give him a crack across the nose, you are teaching the dog that people equate with pain – not a good idea! It is possible to teach your Stafford manners, without losing his enthusiasm for people, although I must repeat that if you want the impeccable manners of a reserved breed such as the German Shepherd, you should not have bought a Stafford in the first place.

OVER-EXUBERANCE

A perennial problem, especially with a young Stafford, is over-exuberance with visitors to your home. One 'solution' is to shut him away whenever a visitor calls, which, of course, is no solution at all – merely an avoidance. If anything, continually being shut away will make the dog even more excited when he is actually able to meet a visitor face to face. Early, firm training while he is still small is the best. Put him down gently but firmly and say "No". The happier and jollier the pup's character, the more persistent he is likely to be and so the more determined you must be. Do not lose your temper, but keep on and do not give up until your pup has four feet on the ground. It is a great help if you can get the co-operation of your visitors. Nothing will undermine your authority more than your visitor asserting 'I don't mind if he jumps up' or 'I've got my old trousers on so he can do what he likes'. Other people will object to having fingers nipped or stockings laddered – the pup will not know the difference and, once again, it is confusing for him to have different sets of rules for different occasions. In general, the more people he meets, especially when he is small, the quicker he will learn to greet them politely.

TIGERS UNDER THE BED

Around nine to twelve months of age a few Staffords, especially male ones, can develop a sudden fear or reluctance to do certain things that they may have done without any qualms before. They may suddenly develop an aversion to passing through a certain doorway, crossing a bridge, taking a certain pathway. Careful handling of this situation is required. Try to be matter-of-fact and, if possible, think of a special reward. Park the car, which he will very probably love to go in, by the front or back door he does not

Your Stafford must learn to walk on a loose lead.

want to go through. He may crawl a bit but he will go through in the end. One lady I know had a dog who developed a sudden dislike for crossing a metal bridge near her house. By chance, he had a stud job on the other side of this hated bridge – he crossed with alacrity following this sexual encounter. This sort of behaviour is fairly uncommon in Staffords but certainly can occur at the adolescent stage of development and it is important to deal with it as soon as possible before it becomes a fixed characteristic.

LEAD TRAINING
Walking on the lead without pulling is a lesson which must be learned if you do not want to develop one arm longer than the other. Any Stafford will start off his walk with exuberance, but after a hundred yards or so, you should check him back sharply and refuse to proceed if he pulls. Again, this will take patience and determination on your part, but it is worthwhile. The traditional and safest method of controlling a Stafford is on a collar and lead – leather or nylon – which can be wrapped around your hand, as keeping a Stafford on a short lead is often necessary. At training

classes he may be required to wear a choke chain but these are not considered safe for a Stafford on normal walks. Chain or part-chain leads are very cruel to your hands and prevent proper handling of the lead.

Staffords who chew the lead should be chastised, and a little bitter apple or similar spray on the lead may help to discourage them.

Some people find that the only way to stop their Stafford pulling is to use a harness. Personally I dislike these, because you have lost the quick check via the neck which is usually so effective. However, if you find the harness to be your only solution to pulling, please buy the plain leather or nylon harnesses. Flashy metal studded and silvered shielded leather harnesses are the traditional dress of the fighting dog and if you put your Stafford in one of these, do not be surprised if you come in for a lot of rude remarks and frightened stares from the public.

Start teaching the Recall in a confined area.

RECALL

It is most important that pup will come back to you when called. Take a favourite tidbit and when

Remember to show lots of enthusiasm when your dog gets it right.

he comes back to you, reward and praise him. If you are having problems, the extending lead can be very useful – let the pup run to the extent of the lead, call him

back and then reward. With this set-up you will feel confident that your puppy cannot run away, and confidence is the key to success with most dog training exercises.

However frustrated you may feel, never chastise a dog that eventually comes back. This is self-defeating as he will associate coming back with being smacked. The first few times you test a pup about coming back, choose a very quiet area so that there is no chance of distraction. When you are fairly confident that he will come back to you, try him in a busier place. If the young dog appears reluctant to come back, running after him will only encourage him to go further away. Calling his name and actually walking in the opposite direction will often be just the jolt necessary to make the Stafford realise that you are leaving him, and bring him hurtling back to your side.

Training sessions should be viewed as fun.

With a Stafford, be very careful of temptations such as sheep, which are silly creatures that positively beg to be chased. Never trust a Stafford near sheep unless he has grown up with them. Again, the extending lead, which will give the dog some freedom but allow you final control, can be extremely useful.

Chasing a ball is a useful game to teach your Stafford. At a very

Agility training provides mental stimulation as well as physical exercise.

young age, start with a screwed-up piece of paper. A Stafford that loves his ball will be more easily distracted from another dog. Furthermore, the best type of exercise for a Stafford is intensive – ten minutes of sustained running swiftly after a ball is worth ten miles of road work.

In the final analysis it must be said that there are many Staffords who cannot be let off the lead in safety in any public place, for fear they may fall out with another dog. Be responsible and keep such dogs on the lead. They not only get themselves a bad name when they get into fights, but they bring the breed into disrepute as well.

DOG AGGRESSION

With the Stafford there is the additional problem of keeping them from getting into arguments with other dogs. All breeds of dog can be aggressive, but never underestimate the damage that your Stafford can do if he gets into a fight. The quietest can be the most lethal in a fight, never wanting to give up. The golden rule is to guard your pup and young Stafford from being attacked by another dog. If this does happen, in all probability the young Stafford will beat a hasty retreat, but he will not forget. Once he feels confident enough of his own powers he will not back down and, indeed, may well seek out any dog that reminds him of his original tormentor with the aim of striking the first blow this time. A young Stafford who has never had a bad confrontational experience can grow into a confident adult who 'minds his own business' throughout his life. This is what you should aim to achieve.

5 The Adult Stafford

Most dogs do not drop to one meal a day until around eighteen months to two years of age. The amount and type of food must vary with the individual dog and your lifestyle. No two animals are exactly alike, and a diet that may suit one will not necessarily benefit another. It is a matter of getting to know your dog.

ADULT DIET

There is a basic meat plus biscuit diet. The meat can be raw or cooked. Tripe is a favourite with many dog breeders and, although the smell is horrendous, raw green tripe is one food that will set any dog's mouth watering! I do not advise feeding tripe to any animal under six months of age. Meat in sausage form – rabbit, chicken, beef and lamb flavoured – is easy to keep fresh, but many people prefer canned foods for ease of storage and serving. There is a multitude of canned foods available including supermarket own-brands.

Meat, in whatever form, should be fed with biscuit. Some of the more expensive varieties of canned food are very rich and, if your dog cannot cope with these, try the cheaper types which he may find easier to digest.

Finally there is a large range of complete, dry foods. Unfortunately, because they do not look like protein, there is a tendency for some people to use them like biscuit and add them to meat. In fact, they are usually very high in protein and should be fed strictly according to the instructions. Remember when feeding dry foods that ample water must be available to the dog at all times. Dogs vary, and while one Stafford may thrive on this type of food, another may flourish only on canned food. The proof of the pudding is in the condition of your dog – does his coat shine, his eyes look bright, and are his motions firm?

FOOD SUPPLEMENTS

If you are feeding a meat and biscuit diet you may need to give additives in the form of cod liver oil or vitamin tablets but if you are feeding a canned or complete diet, beware of additives. It is possible to over-vitaminise and this may cause damage to bones and joints in the growing dog – so read the instructions on your packets and cans with care.

All the best proprietary brands of dog food have excellent advisory services, so do not be afraid to write to them for advice should you have problems. It is not a bad thing to add some gravy and table scraps in small quantities to a dog's dinner, but one word of warning. 'Adding the household scraps' can grow into a full-scale 'he won't eat anything unless it's what we are eating' syndrome. This is wasteful and may be harmful to the dog.

FUSSY EATERS

It must be said that some Staffords are finicky eaters. You

You will learn with experience what is the correct weight for your dog.

really must be firm. Pick up the leftover food, throw it away, and start again the next day. Daily changes of diet and showing concern will only encourage the problem until it becomes a battle of wits between you and the dog. It should be noted that poor eaters very rarely occur in large families of dogs – the knowledge that there is another animal ready to eat the food is a great stimulant to appetite.

A young pup who is a poor eater should be checked for worms as these can inhibit appetite.

THE IDEAL WEIGHT

A fat Stafford is not a pretty sight. A Stafford should have a waist, i.e. immediately behind his ribs his body should shape inwards. He should have a covering over his ribs, but one should be able to press the sides of the dog and make contact with the bones of the ribs.

There is a popular cult among some Stafford owners to 'strip out' their dogs so that they present a very lean, highly muscled, 'macho' silhouette. In extreme cases you can count the ribs and the knobs of the spine. Such owners claim that this dog is 'fighting fit' and this is how the Stafford should look. Of course the dogs may have looked like this in the old fighting days, but, even then, the dog would only have been held at that weight for a short period of time – six weeks' preparation, the fight, and then relaxation. No one would expect an athlete to stay at his performance weight all the time – he trains to that weight and then has a lay-off period.

Keeping a dog stripped down to his lowest possible weight greatly increases his activity. He is like a coiled spring, feeling so keyed-up that he will be ready to jump out of his skin. Such dogs are almost impossible to live with in the normal confines of a family home, while, outside, they could be a positive danger. So do not be tempted to strip your dog out like this. If you want to live comfortably with your Stafford, keep him at a healthy, but not extreme, weight. A dog who is having a great deal of exercise will need more food, especially carbohydrates, than one who is having the minimum.

To a large extent, the physical well-being of your dog will be fairly obvious. If he is too thin or too fat, you will see that he is

The Stafford's short coat needs little grooming.

lethargic, that his eyes and coat look dull or that he is rarely relaxed and at peace within the home.

GROOMING

Staffords need very little grooming indeed. An occasional brush with a stiff bristle brush to remove loose, dead hair, and an occasional bath, is all that is generally required. Staffords' coats can be made especially shiny with an occasional treat of an oily fish e.g. a can of pilchards, sardines or a cod-liver oil capsule. Stroking and fussing also brings up a good

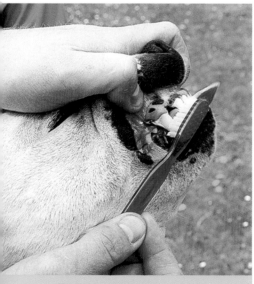

Teeth should be cleaned on a regular basis.

shine on the coat. Bathing them too often removes the natural oils but obviously they can become smelly, and it may be refreshing to have a very occasional bath.

Use baby shampoo or a proprietary dog shampoo. Beware of getting soap in the dog's eyes and always make sure you dry him well – especially the underside of the belly which is virtually hairless. This part of the body should also be dried thoroughly when your Stafford has been out in the rain.

TEETH

It is now very fashionable to recommend a strict teeth cleaning regime for dogs. The second teeth have to last the dog for life. As far as I know, we do not as yet fit canine dental plates, and a lot of our modern dog foods are very soft. An occasional bone or synthetic alternative can be used to keep the tartar down on a dog's teeth.

We clean our dogs' teeth fairly regularly using human toothpaste, which I am assured by my vet works as well for dogs as for us. Many dogs do not like the taste of this nor the way our toothpaste foams, so your dog may prefer a specially formulated canine toothpaste.

EARS

Ears do not normally cause many problems for the Stafford since the rose ear, unlike the fully-dropped ear, allows plenty of air to circulate. Occasionally a dog has very narrow ear canals which cause wax and mites to build up giving off an unpleasant mousy smell. Do not be tempted to pour anything into the dog's ear nor to poke the ear with a cotton bud. Your vet can supply excellent ointment and the debris that floats to the top can then be cleared away from the entrance to the ear.

Nails can be clipped with guillotine nail-clippers.

NAILS

A healthy dog will naturally wear down his nails, especially if given some walking every day on hard surfaces. A puppy should have had his nails cut at an early stage to protect his mother's undercarriage so keep up the idea that feet are there for you to touch, and examine them every week. That way, if you have to cut the adult dog's nails, you are more likely to be able to do this without trauma. Many Staffords hate having their nails cut and, although I would not expect them to bite, they certainly will struggle and become upset as soon as they see the clippers. It may even become necessary to get tranquillisers or similar from the vet, so if you can avoid making an issue of this, so much the better. Some breeders find their animals take more kindly to the use of a rasp file to keep the nails short.

HEALTH CARE

Staffords are generally considered very healthy dogs. As we can see from their past history, it really has been the survival of the fittest and toughest, a high standard which responsible breeders attempt to maintain. However, the breed is not immune to disease and will need annual boosters for the usual canine diseases.

Since Staffords can be accident-prone, taking out an insurance

The Stafford is a tough breed, and will suffer few health problems.

policy to cover veterinary bills is a good idea.

TUMMY UPSETS

Tummy upsets are not uncommon in Staffords although they are no more prone to these than any other type of dog. The hardest thing to get across to pet owners, we find, is the need to deny food to the dog for twenty-four hours. During this time water, or better still water and minerals in the form of an electrolytic solution, should be given. Do not be tempted to give milk as this only exacerbates the problem.

Return the dog to normal

feeding by giving it chicken and rice or fish and rice for the next two days. If the symptoms persist, take the dog to the vet. Staffords are very tough and do not always look depressed even when they are seriously ill.

Food allergies are not unknown in the Stafford but these require professional diagnosis when a suitable diet can be devised.

SEASONAL CYCLE
Stafford bitches have their first 'heat' or 'season' between six and nine months of age. They should not be mated before their second season and only then if they appear to be mentally and physically mature, at around eighteen months of age. A bitch in season will bleed for fourteen days or more and the vulva swells. As the season goes on the flow will gradually reduce, the discharge become straw-coloured and the vulva will reduce in size very slightly. It is at this time that the bitch will be most receptive to a dog. Generally, this stage will be reached at around the twelfth to the fourteenth day, but it must be stressed that this is only a guideline.

If we do not want to breed from a bitch we will allow her to have one season, to make sure she is mentally fully-developed, and then we will have her spayed. We have not found this has ever altered the temperament of a bitch – except in the case of the mature, excitable bitch when the operation has calmed her.

Many old bitches have trouble with septic wombs if un-neutered and this problem, called pyometra, can strike very quickly and be very serious, even fatal. Symptoms to look for, if your bitch is not spayed, are listlessness, excessive drinking and possibly, but not always, a mucky or pink discharge. The condition most commonly shows itself shortly after a season.

HEREDITARY DISEASES
Inherited problems in the pedigree dog is a topic that gives rise to heated discussion. Abnormalities affect all dogs, even mongrels, and are never going to be eradicated completely. The problem for pedigree dog breeders is to prevent such abnormalities becoming so bred into a breed as to be almost the norm. Staffords have a good-sized gene pool to work from, so it is not particularly difficult for individual breeders to get themselves out of trouble, once it occurs.

EYE CONDITIONS

Inherited eye conditions have been the main cause for concern. These take two known forms: Persistent Hyperplastic Primary Vitreous (PHPV) and Hereditary Juvenile Cataract. The first appears to vary in severity but can be detected, following specialised tests, at a very young age. Juvenile Cataract manifests itself at about one year and the dog will be blind by the time it is eighteen months to two years old.

Dogs may have PHPV and to all intents and purposes see perfectly – in fact, it is believed some have a form of tunnel vision. In the most severe cases, a cataract may form on one or both eyes.

In the case of Juvenile Cataract both eyes are affected. They become cloudy and finally completely opaque even to the naked eye. Treatment for cataracts is available.

Responsible breeders test their stock before they use them for breeding and only 'clear' animals should be used in any breeding programme. The Kennel Club registration forms state whether that sire and dam are tested. This does not mean that your pup will definitely be clear of the condition but does make it less likely.

LUXATING PATELLAS

Luxating patellas – a condition where the knee joint on the back leg of the dog slips and causes the dog to limp, is also a recorded problem in the Stafford. Signs to look for are the dog favouring one leg above the other, even if it is not limping in a pronounced way. After a time one leg will be much more heavily muscled than the affected leg, because it has been

The veteran deserves special consideration.

doing twice the work. Operations appear to be successful but are expensive. Some European countries routinely test Staffords for this condition.

HIP DYSPLASIA

Hip dysplasia has been reported in the breed, although recent information suggests that while there will be some Staffords with poor hips, it is not a significant problem. Signs to look for are stiffness when getting up, from around the age of nine months. This condition is not detectable by the naked eye. Again, many European countries test for this condition.

EPILEPSY

Epilepsy has also been reported in the breed but, again, not in significant numbers. The hereditary content is not clear as there are many causes for a dog to have fits and there have not been sufficient reported cases in the Stafford for any inherited link to be identified.

THE VETERAN

The older Stafford has its particular problems. Check teeth for tartar and decay which can cause the breath to be horrid. Also check that he is drinking enough. Kidneys may be working less efficiently and if the dog is not drinking enough fluid his breath can become malodorous. Sometimes it is necessary to add water or gravy to an older dog's food, just to ensure that he is having sufficient fluids.

Many older Staffords cannot cope with the diet they enjoyed when young – especially if this has been a high-protein diet. There are several low-protein diets on the market especially designed for the older dog, or you could offer plain boiled lamb and rice, fish and rice, or chicken and rice which is easier to digest.

Supplements can also help the general health of an ageing dog, while your vet can supply pills that will ease the pain and help activity levels of those suffering from arthritis.

Older Staffords can be delightful pets. The average age of a Stafford is ten to twelve years although many live to fourteen or fifteen. As with all dogs, it is the quality of life that is the important factor. Sometimes we have to be honest with ourselves and ask the question: "Are we keeping an old, sick dog alive for their sake, or for ours?"

6

The Show Dog

Breed Standards are the blueprints for any breed of dog and are used as guidelines by breeders and judges. A basic knowledge of the various parts of the Standard can help in the selection of a puppy and will certainly add to your general enjoyment of the breed. Many breed books are too technical for the first-time owner but you can get a fairly good picture of the 'ideal' with reference to very few technical terms.

TEMPERAMENT

The most important clauses of the Breed Standard, for all owners, are those relating to temperament. For the Stafford, these tell us that the dog must be courageous, tenacious, intelligent, bold, fearless, totally reliable and affectionate, especially with children. If your dog fails to live up to these characteristics he has failed the most important test of all. Remember, however, to judge

carefully – fearless and bold does not mean he should attack, without provocation, anything on four legs. I would add a word of warning about children. No dog, of any breed, should ever be left alone, unsupervised, with a baby or toddler as he may find the noise of crying very disturbing. Nor should children be allowed to exercise a fully-grown Stafford unless accompanied by an adult – they are too strong and determined for a child to control.

HEAD

The original Standard of 1935 included a scale of points for each individual part of the dog. In fact, it proved impractical to judge dogs in this way, the essence of a great dog being the balance achieved by the blending of all the desirable characteristics into a pleasing whole. Nevertheless, it is interesting to note that, under that scheme, the highest number of points was given to the head and

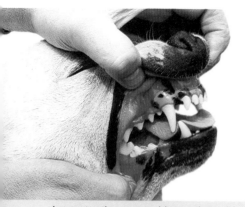

Large teeth arranged in a scissor bite.

neck, which accounted for forty out of the one hundred possible points. By doing this, the founding fathers of the breed drew attention to what is the most distinctive characteristic of the Stafford. Viewed from behind, a dog's breed might be questionable, but, once the dog turns round, you will know for sure that he is a Stafford.

His head is broad, but should not be as massive as the Bulldog. He should have a pronounced stop, or break, in the head which allows his round, but not prominent eyes to look straight ahead. The eyes should be set rather wide apart. His muzzle, although short, should not be less than one third the length of the whole head, and it should be deep

and wide. This gives a strong, bold look to the head but, because the eyes are round and look straight at you, there is a kindness and honesty about his expression. A good Stafford has prominent cheek bumps and a very powerful jaw. Another distinctive characteristic of the Stafford head is the pronounced indentation down the middle of the skull, which is formed by the muscular development. The ideal type of ears are called 'rose' where the ear is folded neatly at the side of the head, the top of the ears being level with the top of the skull. Some Staffords have half-pricked ears which are permissible although not so desirable. Fully-

The head is strong and bold.

pricked or fully-dropped ears are also undesirable.

The Stafford should have large teeth arranged in what is called a scissor bite – that is where the top teeth fit neatly over the bottom teeth. Dentition faults in Staffords are quite common and will be penalised in the show ring, but are only of concern to the pet owner if they prevent normal mastication.

The neck should not be so short that the dog's head appears to be stuck straight on to his body nor as long as that required in most terrier breeds.

The Stafford should appear strong and powerful, but also athletic.

BODY

Overall, the Stafford will present a powerful figure – pound for pound it is probably the strongest dog. But he should not be over-muscled – he is part-terrier and as such should be an active and agile dog. He is a wide-fronted dog, not as broad as the Bulldog but certainly not as narrow as the Whippet or any of the running breeds. He should have strong, straight front legs and very distinctive feet which lay back slightly at the pasterns with a slight turn out at the foot. This, coupled with his well-padded feet, gives the dog enormous purchase power. Staffords which have long feet are referred to as 'hare footed' and usually have very thin pads. Such feet can be a nuisance for pet owners as the dog will not wear down his nails as effectively as the properly constructed foot so cutting, trimming or filing nails becomes a necessary chore. Because he is a wide-fronted breed, the dew claws are not removed from the front legs of a Stafford puppy.

The Stafford is a close-coupled dog, without much length from the end of his ribs to the beginning of his stifles – in other words there is very little unprotected stomach area. He is sturdily built with a nipped-in waist behind a well-sprung and deeply-ribbed body.

The Standard asks the dog to have a 'level topline', which means that his spine is straight and parallel with the ground. In fact there is a discernible little bump just before the tail, which is due to muscle. Avoid a back that dips in the middle like a saddle or one that arches into a hump like a camel.

LEGS

A proper length of leg from elbow to floor, should suggest that he is an athlete and not a couch potato. His hind legs should have a bend at the stifle, or knee joint, and be very well-muscled. His hocks are said to be 'well let down' which means that they will bend towards the ground. In general, a correctly constructed Stafford will stand with his hind legs directly under him – not stretched out behind. Such a stance enables the dog to spring into action without delay – it is no accident that one of the foundation dogs of the breed was called 'Springheeled Jack'.

MOVEMENT

A Stafford has a distinctive movement – not the neat 'stepping on the spot' of many terriers but a forceful, driving motion from behind with a minimum of movement of the front feet. When ambling along, the Stafford will almost roll but, once his pace increases, the back legs move strongly, propelling the dog forward and the front legs stretch out lifting the paws only just off the ground, which conserves his energy and helps him to motor along for a long time at a good speed. His hind legs should not knock together at the hocks, in fact there is a virtual tunnel through his hind and fore legs when he is walking at a smart pace.

Brindle markings can be very dark.

A red Stafford.

COAT

The coat is smooth, short and close to the skin. When in peak condition the coat will shine, aided by a little stiff brushing and body massaging.

TAIL

His tail is set low on his rear and tapers to a point. It should not curl in any way but has a sweeping curve to it, which as the Standard rather poetically tells us 'may be likened to an old-fashioned pump handle'.

The blue colour is more unusual.

COLOURS

Staffords come in a variety of colours. The most common is brindle, which can vary from almost black to mahogany or golden stripes with black. Then there are the reds and fawns. The latter, once extremely popular, are hardly seen today. Any of these colours can come with white – making the pied or skewbald dog.

Pure white is very rarely seen and will carry some colour somewhere on its body. Blue colouring is allowed although this is sometimes difficult to maintain – a deep smoky-coloured pup can become a wishy-washy mushroom-coloured adult.

The only colours that are penalised in the show ring are the liver (i.e. deep, blood red colour)

The Stafford needs little preparation for the show ring.

and the black-and-tan. These undesirable colours occur in all lines of Staffords and are purely a cosmetic fault.

EYES AND NOSE

The Stafford's eyes should be dark and noses and toenails black. Sometimes, the nose will be brown or slate-coloured and the eyes yellow or even green. These variations will be penalised in the show ring. Where a Stafford has white on his feet it is permissible for the toenails to be pink.

Tiny pied puppies often have pink noses when first born. These should gradually become black as the days go by. Failure to become completely black produces a two-tone pink and white 'butterfly'

nose which is also penalised in the show ring.

The rims of the eye should be dark but where the dog has white around the eye it is common to have a pink eye rim.

SIZE

The size of the Stafford causes more argument than any other single characteristic. Big is often used indiscriminately to describe either a heavy dog or a tall dog. It is sometimes forgotten that the range in size of the Bulldogs of the last century was enormous. I have a print of two dogs, Old Storm and Young Storm, who were reputedly 70lbs in weight, but from the same period I have a print of a bitch named Beech said to weigh only 28lbs.

The height at the withers given for the present Standard is between 35.5–40.5cms (14–16 ins) for both sexes. The weights given in the Standard are 12.7–17kgs (28–38lbs) for dogs and 11–15.4kgs (24–34lbs) for bitches. In practice, with modern feeding, many Staffords will weigh more than this.

ENTIRE DOGS

All male animals of whatever breed are required by Kennel Club

Standards to have two fully-descended testicles. If your male Stafford has only one or even no visible testicles, veterinary advice should be obtained as a retained testicle could turn cancerous in later life.

DOG SHOWS

Dog shows sometimes get a bad press, which is unfair since they provide an absorbing hobby for many hundreds of people. Staffords have one great advantage over many other breeds in that they need no real preparation for showing. There is no special trimming or stripping required as in most of the terrier breeds. It is a good idea to make sure he is clean – especially if he has any white on him, and that his coat is shining, then put on a collar and lead and you are ready to go. There is a belief that a special comradeship exists at Stafford shows that is not found in other breeds. Certainly, it is so easy to show a Stafford that many people have gone on to have very successful show careers with animals that they originally bought as pets.

If you decide to show your dog, do so because you want a day out and would like to learn more about the breed. Beware of the chap you meet on your walk who raves about your Stafford and assures you he is a certain champion. Be prepared to lose as well as to win – even the best dogs have bad days or do not appeal to some judges. No Stafford I know has ever won prizes at every show of the season and you have to be prepared to smile when you lose as well as to celebrate when you win.

Selecting a puppy for showing is not easy – hence the number of pet purchasers who later find that they have got the pick of the litter! Experienced breeders will have an idea of the quality of their litter, and should be prepared to tell you which they think are definitely pets – they may have dental or conformation faults which may not be obvious to you. But no experienced breeder will sell you an eight-week-old 'show dog'. There are too many things that can go wrong as the pup grows to maturity.

7 Breeding Staffords

The two most common reasons for pet owners deciding to have a litter from their bitch is that they want an animal just like her to carry on when she is gone, or that they have been told that it is good for a bitch to have at least one litter. The majority of the bitches we have bred have lived as pets, been spayed and never had puppies. I have not found that these have been any less healthy or happy than those who have had a litter. Trying to replicate a dog is not possible nor is it kind to the second animal, who is forever living in the shadow of its predecessor. Better to go back to the person from whom you bought your original dog and see if there had been a repeat mating or a mating from close relatives – this is actually more likely to produce a similar character than mating your bitch to a stud dog whose character you know nothing about.

If you are intent upon having a litter, you have to consider the cost. There will be a stud fee, you will have to provide special accommodation for the bitch and puppies, if there are problems there could be heavy vet fees, and the puppies will need costly food and plenty of it. If they do not find new homes quickly, you will have to keep them while they are eating more and more.

You should also be prepared to take back any pup that you have bred if the animal falls on hard times and needs re-homing.

ASSESSING THE PARENTS

If you are still of a mind to breed, you must make an assessment of your bitch. You will probably need some experienced help to give you an honest opinion of the faults and the virtues of your bitch. If she suffers from any hereditary defect or if she is bad-tempered and unreliable with human beings, it would be totally wrong to breed from her at all.

Make sure that she is healthy and not overweight, that her injections are up-to-date and that she has been wormed and I would advise that you have her eyes tested, all before she is actually mated.

Then, take yourself around to the shows and look for dogs that are strong in the characteristics in which your bitch fails. Try to handle any dog that you like to assure yourself that you are likely to get puppies of the correct temperament.

CHOOSING A STUD DOG

When you have made up your mind about a stud dog, approach the owner and ask if he would be willing to let you use his dog, and enquire about the stud fee. You should do this long before your bitch actually comes into season.

It is usual to pay the stud dog owner a fee, although occasionally he may ask for a puppy instead. The decision is yours, and if you do not wish to hand over one of the puppies, do not agree to this arrangement. It is of the greatest importance that you settle the business part of the transaction before you allow your bitch to be mated. The stud dog owner must sign the Kennel Club stud form –

which you will retain and use to register the puppies. If you have an unsatisfactory mating it is possible for you to withhold the fee, and the stud dog owner to withhold the form, until it is certain that the bitch is in whelp. Remember that you are paying for the service, not for puppies or a certain number of live puppies. However, there is usually a gentleman's agreement that if your bitch does not produce puppies after she has been served, a free stud service will be provided on the next season. You may not go to two dogs in the one season. Once a dog has entered a bitch, it is a Kennel Club rule that the name of that dog must appear as the sire of the puppies. If you are dissatisfied with the mating, and go to another dog in that same season, both dogs' names must appear on the registration form as the sires of the puppies. The reason for this is that a dog produces millions of sperm and even the shortest of unions can produce puppies.

I have made no mention of using a pet as a stud dog. In general, breeders wanting to improve their stock are unlikely to use an unshown pet dog. From the pet owner's point of view, a dog not used for stud is less likely to run off after bitches in season than one who has been used. It is therefore to your advantage to leave the handsome fellow in blissful ignorance.

MATING

It is normal for the bitch to visit the stud dog and for the organisation of the mating to be in the hands of the stud dog owner. One area where I would advise you to object is if the stud dog owner has the old-fashioned notion of performing an internal examination of your bitch. This is a sure way to introduce infection and could well result in damage to your bitch.

A Stafford bitch may show a token resistance to a male, especially if it is her first mating but sustained resistance suggests that you have got the incorrect day or that she is not meant to be mated at all. Even bitches who are normally fierce with other dogs, if their hormones are right, will have an overwhelming desire to get themselves mated.

Normally the dogs will tie – that is, the bitch will hold the dog's penis by a reflex action of her internal muscles. Owners of Stafford stud dogs and brood

The stud dog should be selected to complement the bitch's qualities.

bitches generally like to obtain a tie, although it is perfectly possible to produce a litter without having this tie. The animals will turn back to back and stay like this for anything from five to thirty-five minutes. You will be expected to restrain your bitch during this time, although there should be no aggression shown during this period.

CARE AFTER MATING

Once your bitch has been mated she will be keener than ever to go out and look for another mate. It is beyond question therefore that you must guard your bitch. Keep her in your safe garden, as secure after the mating as you did before.

A sound temperament is essential in all dogs chosen for breeding.

A bitch may be mated up to the twenty-first or twenty-second day from the onset of bleeding. Watch to see all swelling goes down and give her a good wash before taking her out for a walk or letting her near male dogs.

If a misalliance should occur with your bitch at any time, no amount of water-throwing will cause the tie to break – it is a reflex action and you may do your bitch and the dog serious harm if you try to break the tie forcibly. Be patient, wait till the tie breaks and then contact your vet who can give an injection to prevent conception. Do not be tempted to keep a cross-Stafford litter as they can be of unpredictable nature.

THE PREGNANT BITCH

Once your bitch has been mated you should be sure that she is having the best-quality food – but not an increased amount. It is very bad for the bitch if you allow her to get fat during pregnancy. You will find there are recommended quantities for bitches in whelp given with every branded food. You may like to give her a special course of vitamins. More controversial is the question of giving calcium, now considered a possible cause of inertia (inability to have contractions) in some bitches. The most up-to-date advice I could find recommends no calcium additives during pregnancy but a big dosage once whelping starts and some throughout the lactating period i.e. all the time the bitch is feeding the pups.

Consult your vet about worming during pregnancy as there are products on the market which claim to eliminate the larvae as they migrate from the liver, but this must be done at the optimum time during the pregnancy. Many breeders prefer to worm the bitch before mating, assume that the pups will have some worms, and deal with them as soon as possible.

Towards the end of the pregnancy the bitch may well be so big as to be uncomfortable. To ease this discomfort, it is a good idea to split her feed into two small portions. Keep up her exercise, but if, towards the end of her time, she does not want to go quite as far on her walks as usual, respect her wishes.

The normal gestation period is sixty-three days, but again this is only a guide. Perfectly healthy pups can be born at fifty-seven days. Equally, a bitch may go days over the nominal sixty-three. I would advise you to take veterinary advice if the sixty-third day has passed with no signs of birth. Staffords can resist pain to such a degree that, whereas a bitch of another breed would be showing grave signs of discomfort, she may sit fairly happily while everything inside her is going wrong. So check her out once day sixty-three comes, but trust your vet if he advises a 'wait and see' attitude.

Years ago many Staffords were given caesareans, as much to present the owners with six live puppies and keep them quiet as to help the bitch. I sense a change in practice nowadays and can personally say that waiting can bring about the desired result. Caesareans are a source of argument in this breed as in many

others. I have never thought of the Stafford as the easiest breeding machine – probably because my father lost one of my favourite bitches in whelp, when I was a child. I do believe that there is a strong hereditary input here and, if you have a bitch who was herself born from a caesarean, then I think you must expect trouble.

Continuing to breed generation after generation from bad whelpers is the death knell for any breed and is totally unnecessary in the Stafford. There are enough bitches who are good whelpers and excellent mothers for us to discard the others from our breeding programmes.

WHELPING QUARTERS

Buy or make a whelping box for your bitch. This should be cleanable – wooden or plastic – and have a pig rail around at least three sides to stop puppies being squashed against the side. We like a low-fronted box, with additional strips that we can add as the puppies become bigger. Let the bitch get used to the box well before the pups are due and put the box in a convenient room away from other pets where she can feel secure. In the wild she would build a den in a hillside and

Most Stafford bitches will take motherhood in their stride.

it is fairly common for bitches to try to have their first pup outside under a hedge, or similar dark, inaccessible place. The box must be large enough for the bitch to be able to lie on her side, completely stretched out, as this is the best and most efficient way for her to feed her pups.

As a precaution you should have the following ready: hand towel, sterilised scissors, paper towels, hot water bottle with cover, cardboard box, phone number of your vet and a bottle of whisky. The first six are for use with the bitch, the seventh for you – do

not be tempted to give alcohol to a whelping bitch.

Line the box with plenty of paper topped by a Vet-Bed. Beware of using loose blankets, as a pup could get itself entangled and strangle on pieces of cloth. Puppies left on newspaper alone can develop sores and scabs on their front leg as they scrabble for teats.

WHELPING

At the first sign of labour, the bitch will begin to tear up the paper and as the pains increase the tearing become more frantic. She will begin to pant and in general become very distressed. There will be times when everything will quieten down and she may even doze – she is conserving her energy.

Make sure that she goes out to relieve herself and watch her carefully while she is outside, but remain calm and allow her to do pretty well as she likes. Unfortunately, there is no time limit to this first stage, other than to say that it generally lasts longer in a maiden bitch than in one who has had a litter before. If you can see milk coming from her teats then you should have your pups within twenty-four hours. You can always consult your vet's surgery if you are anxious. Call for veterinary attention immediately if there is any sign of a green discharge.

The second stage of the labour commences when the bitch starts to have contractions proper and she will push, trying to expel the puppies. You should not leave a bitch pushing for longer than two hours without seeking help.

Each pup will be born in a sac or membrane attached to a placenta or afterbirth – and you should make sure that you see one for every pup. The bitch will know instinctively that she must bite the cord and she will eat the afterbirth. Should she be too bewildered, then you should cut the cord with scissors – just remember to leave a long cord as the bitch will lick and bite it down during the next two days. Do not be too hasty to 'jump in' and cut the cord. Make sure that the pup's mouth is clear of the membrane and that the puppy is able to breathe, and then wait for the bitch to take her time in chewing the cord. There are various schools of thought about what to do with the afterbirth. Personally, since Stafford litters are not over-large, we let them clean everything up – our philosophy is that the bitch is best left to her own devices. Some people let them eat one or two and then take the rest away.

NEWBORN PUPPIES

The firstborn will attract all the bitch's attention, and she will lick and lick the puppy and may even walk around carrying it. Trying to take the puppy away will only disturb her. So grit your teeth, tell her she is a good girl and hope for the next pup to come quickly. Pups can come after five minutes or after an hour. We would not expect to have more than two hours between births. Once pup number two comes, you can take number one and give it a nice rub with the towel – keeping the pup warm is important. Left to themselves our bitches will gather puppies to their faces, lying on the teats, leaving their rear ends unimpeded as they feel another pup is about to be born. We keep a hot water bottle and cardboard box handy, in case the bitch has an unforeseen problem and has to go the vet, in which case you are ready to keep the pups warm in her absence.

You should note the time a pup is born, and its markings. This way you have good information to tell a vet if required, and it makes a good diary of events for you afterwards. Sometimes a pup is born back legs first and this can cause problems as the shoulders on a Stafford are quite wide. This is where you use your paper towels, firmly holding the pup and pulling in time with the bitch's contractions – down and under her belly.

Warmth is of the utmost importance for newly born puppies. You may feel very warm, but get down on the floor next to your whelping box to make sure that there are no draughts around the pups at this low level.

Knowing when a bitch has finished giving birth is not always easy and many a time an owner has retired to bed only to find another pup in the box next day. You can palpate her, if you can persuade her to stand up and let you gently feel her sides. Generally she will relax, accept a small drink and lay back to let all the pups feed – which she may not have allowed during the actual birth. The average litter size for Staffords is five to six.

POST-WHELPING CARE

Staffords are generally very good about letting you touch their puppies and you may, by this time, have an idea how many of each sex you have. But once all the litter is born, it is best to leave the bitch to her little family without interference from you.

You should encourage her to go outside and relieve herself – indeed you may actually have to carry her outside and you will find that as soon as she can, she will run in again, probably whimpering to herself in her concern to get back to the litter. We take the opportunity while she is away, to replace the dirty, wet paper with clean, and if there are any dead or deformed pups we take them out now. If left for more than a day, the bitch will know if there is one missing.

Some bitches like to cover their litter up if they leave them – perhaps only with a piece of paper. In these cases, when she is out we change the paper and bedding, keeping that piece of paper to put back over the pups by the time she returns.

Do not invite friends or neighbours, indeed anyone but the immediate family, to see the litter at this time. Until they are ten days old the puppies are blind and deaf, and completely dependent on their mother. On the whole, Staffords are excellent mothers but if you upset or confuse the bitch's instincts, then you may end up with her laying on them or even killing them.

The day following the birth the bitch may appear a little unsettled, panting and a little wild-eyed. This is quite normal and, in our experience, the more prolonged the birth, the more acute is the reaction. Keeping her whelping quarters quiet and giving a little glucose in her drink of milk can help her to settle.

A not uncommon problem after birth is eclampsia, which is due to

Weaning has started, but the puppies still feed from their mother.

calcium deficiency. Veterinary help is needed but the signs to watch for are extreme discomfort, excessive panting, and a stumbling walk. The bitch may not appear to know where she is and, finally, will collapse.

A lactating bitch must be fed properly to ensure that the puppies thrive and she does not lose too much condition. For the first twenty-four hours a light diet of fish or chicken can help prevent the possibility of diarrhoea caused by the bitch eating the afterbirth.

After that it is essential to provide good-quality protein and plenty of fluids.

WEANING

To help your bitch recover her figure properly you should begin weaning the pups at three weeks, or even a little earlier if the litter is very large. Start with a little milk such as Lactol, Welpie, or baby formula. After about a week begin to introduce the pups to meat, feeding each one by hand if necessary. Gradually increase the number of meals adding cereal to two milk meals and a little soaked small-bite mixer to the two meat meals. The puppies may enjoy scrambled egg, or scrambled egg with cheese, for a change. When they are old enough you may find it more convenient to give special puppy-formula tinned food, or complete foods, according to the number and size of the puppies'

As you gradually increase the number and size of the puppies meals you will find that the bitch's milk will naturally decrease in quantity. There should be no need for you to intervene with milk suppressant tablets unless she is a bitch who makes an inordinate amount of milk. Keep feeling her milk bags during the weeks she is feeding the pups to make sure they are not hard, as this can be an early sign of mastitis and the milk supply will have to be stopped. Hand rearing a litter of pups is not to be recommended unless there is no other option. It is very hard work, totally time consuming, and not the best for the pups anyway. The bitch supplies milk according to demand, and you should be careful of attempting to draw off milk by hand.

As the pups grow, make sure their nails are not scratching the bitch's undercarriage, and cut them with clippers if they are too long. During the first few weeks of life you may like to weigh your pups – this will reassure you that the pups are actually thriving. They should weigh, on average, one pound for every week of their

Puppies spend a lot of time sleeping.

lives
i.e. at three
weeks three
pounds, at seven
weeks seven
pounds, etc.

If a bitch discards a puppy while caring normally for the rest of the litter, beware of this puppy. Bitches have an instinct for the faulty pup, and many times I have known people hand – rear a discarded pup only to find, when it is old enough to have a character and they are attached to it, that in fact it is malformed and will have to be humanely destroyed to prevent further suffering.

Puppies will soon know that you are food providers. Individual feeding may be necessary if you have a wide variation in size. We find that, after four to five weeks of age, circular metal puppy

Increasingly, the litter becomes more independent.

feeders are excellent as you can place the food in appropriate piles and each pup has a fair chance of eating his correct portion. All puppies should be monitored when they are being fed to make sure that they are eating properly and getting the proper amounts.

Stafford mothers are tough with their pups. I once had a terrified neighbour banging on my front door saying "your dog is killing her pups". In fact, it is her way of training the pups. She may even pick on one in particular – usually the one that 'answers her back' the most.

Puppies do not like to foul their beds, even at a young age. If you arrange the blanket so that there is a small space with only paper on the floor, you will find that they will drag themselves off the blanket and perform on the paper. Bitches will clean up after their puppies until the pups are weaned then, I am sorry to say, it is all down to you. Keeping puppies clean and sweet is a full-time job and if you have not the time nor the commitment, this is yet another reason to think twice about the advisability of having a litter.

WORMING

Puppies should be wormed at two to three weeks and no later. There are simple, liquid forms of wormer that are easy to give at this early age. Because the bitch has been clearing up after them, remember it will be necessary to worm her as well. The pups will need to be wormed at least twice more before they go to their new homes at around eight weeks of age. Always weigh the puppies and follow the instructions exactly.

FINDING HOMES

If you have used a stud dog belonging to a well-known breeder you may find that he or she will forward enquiries for puppies. Otherwise you should use the facilities of your local breed club. Always check carefully before you let a puppy go to a new home and, if in doubt, hold back and do not let the puppy go.

Remember to send your stud form off to the Kennel Club, with the details of your puppies, as soon as you can. Then you will have registration forms as well as pedigrees, diet sheet etc. to give to the new owners.